A CHRISTIAN LOOKS AT
THE JEWISH QUESTION

A CHRISTIAN LOOKS AT THE JEWISH QUESTION

BY

JACQUES MARITAIN

LONGMANS, GREEN AND CO.

NEW YORK · TORONTO

1939

FOREWORD

This essay is the development of a lecture given in Paris on February 5, 1938, at the *Théâtre des Ambassadeurs*, under the auspices of the *Groupes Chrétienté*, and afterwards delivered by the author, with some additions which new events required, before the American public in New York, on December 14, 1938, at the Cosmopolitan Club, under the auspices of the National Conference of Jews and Christians.

I am indebted to Mr. A. S. Oko, Dr. Emmanuel Chapman and Dr. Harry McNeill, for the revision they have made of the English text, and I here express my sincere gratitude to them, as well as to the publishers, who have been kind enough to publish this small book, revised and augmented according to a situation which is still in a state of flux.

PARIS, *April 5, 1939*

A CHRISTIAN LOOKS AT
THE JEWISH QUESTION

I should like to speak, in this short essay, of the Jewish question and the situation of the Jews in the world of today.   I shall treat this vast and distressing topic, conscious of my own inadequacy, but at least with all the insight which my reason and my faith can convey, and I shall treat it with that spirit of independence which we are determined to defend as our last possession.

I shall speak first of the special problems connected with situations in certain countries, out of which anti-Semitism is making capital; then of the dispersion of Israel from the viewpoint of its divine significance, and at the same time, of the problem of anti-Semitism considered in its spiritual essence.

In a third section, I shall deal briefly with factual questions of particularly grave urgency, that is to say, of the tragic situation in which the Jews at present find themselves in certain parts of Europe.

1

I

SPECIFIC ASPECTS OF THE PROBLEM

Let us consider, as briefly as possible, the concrete problems which make the Jewish question particularly acute, not so much among us, but in those countries which may be put into one of two categories: countries with a Jewish minority of considerable size, and countries, like Germany, where the great catastrophe following the war has been primarily diverted onto the heads of the Jews.

Countries with a Large Jewish National Minority

In countries with a large Jewish national minority, it is obvious that the presence of an ethnic mass with its own traditions, schools and tongue, creates a special problem concerning civil life and the general welfare of the State.   This is true even in a country like Poland, which formerly welcomed the Jews with respect, and on several occasions invited them to furnish it with a middle class of artisans and traders, and in whose national culture the Jewish rôle has been considerable.   And this problem is more or less seriously complicated when, to the long-established Jewish population of a country, is added a wave of more recent immigrants. As a matter of fact, the figures of Polish and Rumanian anti-Semites regarding these more recent immigrations seem considerably exaggerated. Nevertheless, the problem exists, simply as a particular case of the problem of national minorities, whose fate in contemporary Europe is often so cruel. In certain circumstances, especially where the Jews do not fit into the political scheme of the community, it can become extremely irritating.

But I maintain that anti-Semitism *makes impossible* any solution of the concrete difficulties encountered in such cases. Not only does it falsify by exaggeration the factual data, but it removes the preliminary conditions required for any practical solution. For specific solutions are conceivable only in an atmosphere of mutual understanding and collaboration, and the disease of anti-Semitism destroys the state of mind necessary in the very first place for such understanding on both sides; on the one, directly, and on the other by the passions of protest and resentment which it provokes in response, so that exasperation and misunderstanding, like reciprocal evils, grow irremediably in the minds of both parties.

Instead of offering proper political solutions to problems of a political order, anti-Semitism, even that so-called political anti-Semitism of which I am speaking at the moment, brings to bear on these problems already falsified beyond recognition, solutions that are themselves false: laws of discrimination and measures of persecution inducing or designed to induce total emigration, which is, moreover, impossible.

It is not simply a confession of low vitality for a State to resort to the extermination of certain levels of its population which it deems itself incapable of adapting to the service of the commonwealth. It means also the preparation of future hardships because it signifies the lowering, by just so much, of internal energies, whose positive expression might have overcome those crises which receive only an apparent cure from a surgical operation not even aseptic but, in fact, infected with hate and injustice.

For the justification of such false or illusory solutions, so-called political anti-Semitism employs a set of arguments which have no rational validity, but which have great emotional force, and which slip furtively over into racial anti-Semitism. Indeed, from recent Jewish immigrants whom alone it first pretends to attack, it extends little by little to Jews long established in the land, and to assimilated Jews, even to converted Jews; in short, to Jews as such, against whom it finally raises the racial myth. Let us say a few words about these arguments, which anti-Semitic propaganda is trying to popularize universally.

The Jews, it is said, crowd into a certain number of lucrative professions, notably the so-called liberal professions. Let them be driven out! That will mean a certain percentage of competitors out of the way. There is the danger, however, that they will be replaced by other competitors, springing from the undesirable multiplication of humanity — even of non-Jewish humanity — who will thus threaten, dear anti-Semites, by their baneful existence, not only your honest livelihood but also your innate sense of justice and of unselfish, spiritual, Western values. Into the bargain, it is plain that the Jews, unless one wants them all to die of hunger, must earn their living in some calling, and naturally they will be more numerous in those which suit them best. The world will forgive a natural irritation with successful competitors, provided it stays within reason; but what arises here is clan hatred. Wherever the Jews are they will be considered superfluous. What is really being denied them is purely and simply the right to exist.

Let us pass by those voluntary agreements which, in a really organic (pluralist) régime, could be reached with the Jewish community.* If you want to free certain professions of the Jewish influx, the best thing would be to endeavor to man them yourselves by demonstrating more working intelligence and diligence than the Jews, and by fighting, through legitimate professional organization, the abuses of free competition, whatever their source.

In this way competition between Jews and non-Jews would stimulate a raising of the cultural level, whereas recourse to the brutal practice of the *numerus clausus,* let alone the *numerus nullus,* equally humiliating for non-Jews and for Jews, tends in itself to lower the level.

* See further pages 34–35.

It is also said that Jews are given to usury, monopoly, white slavery, and pornographic literature. Thus they appear to be the pernicious tempters of native populations, whose Christian ardor and virtues are painted for us by our novelists, newspaper gossip columns, and police-court reports. Because of their press and publications, the Jews are responsible for the immorality sweeping over the populace. The Jews go in for dishonest political activities; they are, of course, Communists, their extensive rôle in the ranks of ultra-right terrorist organizations not yet having been exposed.

"The Jews" — it is very natural for a man, especially some literary man or businessman on whom one or two Jews have played a shabby trick, or who has noticed among the large number of questionable personalities which life has placed upon his path, a few with Semitic profiles among the many unclassifiable — it is so natural for a man to say, not *"a Jew,"* or *"three Jews,"* or *"ten Jews"* with whom I have had dealings are this or that, but *"the Jews"* (of whom there are 16 million in the world), *"the Jews"* are this or that. It is so natural, — but it is hardly rational.

These summary turns of speech lead naturally to the worst of sophistries. "The Jews," runs the anti-Semitic contention, commit such and such crimes. What sense is there in attributing to an entire community the individual faults of *some* of its members? If, moreover, certain social evils, such as usury in some agricultural countries, are, as a result of national historical conditions, attributable especially to the Jews, in the case of other social evils which the anti-Semitic argument blames on "the Jews," non-Jews have revealed themselves as brilliant competitors, not to speak of still further categories of social evils (such as alcoholism, crimes of violence, etc.), in which non-Jews clearly eclipse the Jews. Evil is done not by *"the Jews,"* but by *some* Jews, and also by *some* non-Jews. What is the use of burdening one's conscience by transgressing, in the case of the Jews, the elementary rules of law and of civilized life? The social body must defend itself energetically against evils facing it, against a slanderous and corrupt press, against degrading publications, yes! The only effective way is to crush, if necessary by Draconian laws, all offenses and abuses, no matter who has committed them; but not to strike a mass of innocents for the offenses and abuses committed by some of their brethren, and by others than their brethren, and which would always find votaries even if all the Jews were exterminated.

Finally, as for the propagation of false ideas and false moral maxims, there would be reason to praise heaven if *"the Jews"* (*some Jews*) were the only ones responsible! We know very well that this is not the case, and that in the grand total the contribution made by non-Jews is far greater than that of the Jews. Mr. Julius Streicher and the instigators of pogroms are not Jews, and thus they spoil a powerful confirmation of their own argument, which imputes to the Jewish race all the scourges of humanity. Messrs. Rosenberg, Goebbels, and Hitler, and the other armed disrupters of Western civilization are not Jews; Lenin was not one, nor is Stalin; and even our vociferous French novelist, Mr. Céline, who before massacring people in bad books, wrote long ago *Voyage au bout de la Nuit*, is no Jew, although he seems to have journeyed to the end of the night only to find there the Protocols of Zion which awaited him, deposited in those filthy shadows by the former Tsarist police.

I just spoke of the Protocols of Zion.   Everybody is aware that in Germany the Hitler propaganda machine makes systematic use of this alleged document; everybody also knows that this is the most impudent of forgeries, as has been proved by all those who have seriously studied the question, among others the prominent Jesuit, Father Pierre Charles.   If there remain orators and publicists who still dare to call upon this forgery to spread anti-Semitic legends, one must believe that they have lost respect for their own intelligence and that of those who listen to them.

To charge the Jews with the sins of Bolshevism, to identify Judaism and Communism, is a classic theme of Hitlerite propaganda, which sometimes throws in Catholicism for good measure.   The theme is echoed with admirable discipline by the anti-Semites of all lands.   I do not believe that in general the Jewish spirit, which the same mighty brains reproach with bearing an anarchic fever for liberty, easily adapts itself to Communist conformism.   What is true is that in some countries a section of Jewish youth may find itself driven to revolutionary extremism by the force of persecution. Those primarily responsible, in such cases, are those who make their life unbearable. Thus, in a general way, those primarily responsible for supreme disorder are the false men of order, Jews and non-Jews, who, uniformly preferring injustice to disorder, base order on a fundamental, though at first concealed, disorder, thus offending the very principle of order and the Author of all nature.

We, as much, or more than the anti-Semites (whose fury generally vents itself only on poor Jews), detest the hegemony of banks and finance, whether Jewish or non-Jewish, and no less the rule of money in any form. And here it is the materialistic structure and spirit of the modern world which horrifies us, whoever the individuals, Jews or non-Jews, who find themselves, generally without personal fault, involved in this inhuman structure. We know, moreover, that the great mass of Jews is made up neither of bankers nor of financiers, but of a population struggling against every form of urban poverty.

We do not underestimate the gravity of the great economic difficulties of our epoch and of the general economic crisis of civilization.   We say that it is not by hounding the Jews, but by transforming the economic and social structures, which are the real cause of those difficulties and of that crisis, that we can effectively remedy them.   Anti-Semitism diverts men from the real tasks confronting them.   It diverts them from the true causes of their woes — which lie simultaneously in our egoistic and hypocritical hearts and in the social structures causally interrelated to our moral wretchedness — anti-Semitism diverts men from the true causes of their sufferings to throw them against an innocent multitude, like a worthless crew which, instead of combatting the tempest, would throw overboard some of their companions, until finally they all are attempting to choke each other and set fire to the vessel on which humanity lost in dreams has taken passage.

The German Drama

I have spoken of so-called political anti-Semitism and of the soil on which it falls in some countries with a large Jewish national minority.   As a matter of fact, it is the example and contagion of German racism which for several years has distorted and aggravated, *bewitched* as it were, the conflict in such countries.

A pathetic and unfortunate nation, longing to feel itself possessed of a common soul, the German people is also cast in a historic drama to which nobody with a sense of human solidarity can remain indifferent. Why must it, drawn by one of those magic melodies against which it has no power of resistance, today seek self-realization by trampling on Jews and Christians, — self-realization, and doom? This is not the place in which to expatiate on this drama. I will mention here only what relates to the Jews: if it be true, as the Jewish sociologist, Mr. Arthur Ruppin, says, and as Karl Marx said with greater violence, that there is a sort of affinity and interrelation between the Jewish spirit of adventure and the capitalist spirit of adventure, and if it be true that nowhere is Jewry more at home than in a capitalist civilization; * if, on the other hand, it be true that Germany, and above all post-war Ger-

* Whether we consider free competition, or interest paid on money loans, or price conceived as the result of discussion rather than as the expression of the objective value of a commodity ("just price"), we see ideas related to Jewish (and more generally to Oriental) economic conceptions, which the change from the medieval guild régime to the capitalist régime rendered predominant.

many, is the European country which has best
known the wretched euphoria and the spiritual ver-
tigo of a disoriented capitalism, one is less aston-
ished by the paradox that, in Germany, an unprecedented tempest of hate has suddenly risen against
the Jews, not to the extent that the Jews remained
aloof but, on the contrary, to the extent that they
became assimilated, substantially assimilated to the
German community to the point of playing a major
rôle in German culture and literature as such, and
of sometimes forgetting the Jewish people and the
woes of Israel.   It is as though modern Germany
sought, in her innermost being, to punish her own
bad conscience in the person of the Jews, a stupefied
scapegoat who cried out in vain: "But I live only for
the power and glory of Germany; I worship you
alone, German greatness and German force in the
service of a civilization entirely dedicated to the
conquest of power."

The intensely and morbidly industrialized German civilization, deeply penetrated by the spirit of
modern capitalism, after a crushing military de-
feat, arrived at general moral bankruptcy together
with frightful material misery of the poor classes.

In this people the poisons of humiliation have been nurtured and stored up. This civilization, neither finding nor even seeking an inner creative principle of a fundamentally new order, chose, instead of the Communist revolutionary catastrophe toward which its internal logic drove it, another revolutionary catastrophe which at least saved the State while losing everything else. It is not at all surprising that, entering thereafter upon a general régime in which illusion, myth and prestige replace and devour, as in an operation of black magic, the forms and functioning of real causes, this régime should instinctively give a special place to the anti-Jewish myth, which endows any fool with a means of explaining the misfortunes of history and of shifting on to somebody *guilty of everything*, the burden of his anguish and of his unhappy memories.

But if what I have just said is accurate, there is reason to believe that the relations between Germany and her Jews are more complex than appears. For neither the former nor the latter has changed — I mean really and basically. However persecuted, however humiliated, however abominably trodden under foot they may be, the majority of German

Jews continues to cherish Germany, at least the Germany of the 19th century. As they weep by the waters of Babylon, it is not Zion which they recall, but pre-Führer Berlin, the Berlin of great capitalist adventure, of sublime intercourse with a worldly prince who had not yet donned the brown shirt of racial austerity. And, on the other hand, the Germany of Hitler, in seeking to reject Israel, has embraced the very worst of Israel. I mean that sentiment of racial pride which is, in some carnal Jews, the naturalistic corruption of the supernatural idea of divine election. The racists are indebted to the Old Testament, as the Communists are to the New. It is the Scriptures of the Jews from which the former drew, only to corrupt it, the idea of a chosen people, a people of God; it is the Gospel from which the latter received, only to denature it, the idea of universal salvation and human brotherhood.

What I have just said must be well understood. I do not reproach the German Jews, as some have so inopportunely, because they have not profited by Nazi persecution to be converted to Christianity. I realize that they have not emulated their ancestors of the time of the prophets, have not sufficiently understood the cry of their suffering to turn toward *their God*, and to remember *their origins*, which were in Abraham, Isaac and Jacob. Whether in Germany or out of it, they seem to have offered as a response to the terrible scourge which German racism has brought on the Jews, nothing but quite justifiable complaints and justifiable indignation, supplemented only by a call for an American boycott of German products and an appeal to international humanitarian literature. But that impulse of the heart which penetrates to the secret roots of history, that resurrection of spiritual forces in the face of which persecutors cannot stand and always end by admitting what they are, a bit of straw and blood-stained mud, can it be that Israel, surprised and perhaps paralyzed by its rationalism, no longer knows how to, or dares to put its trust in such a power?

Jews and Christians are curiously at one here. When they think of the state of affairs in Germany before 1933, are they not led to ask whether here, as in other lands, but with more immediately tragic consequences, there was not in too many of them

a lack of a certain humbly human compassion regarding those elementary realities whose terrible importance for our times has recently been indicated?
Each in their respective way privileged by divine
adoption, did they not both too tranquilly carry
on *their business,* their business of earth and their
business of heaven?   Did they not fail to observe
with sufficient sorrow the countenance of men and
of the world degenerating before their very eyes,
did they not fail to live close enough to the misery
of men and of the world?

It is, after all, a new face, the somberly ardent
face of pagan might which is revealing itself in
men.   I do not wish to speak of these matters without paying tribute of admiration and brotherly love
to the Christians of Germany, Catholics and Prot-
estants alike, who suffer persecution like the Jews,
and who are defying all dangers to defend against
blasphemous rage both the Gospel and the Old
Testament.   Perhaps it is not commonly known,
but the fact is that a great many priests are now suffering — and frightfully — in concentration camps.
The bond of suffering in persecution has led both
Christians and Jews to a consciousness of the fun-

damental bond uniting men, if not in their doctrine and rule of life, at least in that single origin which fashions them all in the image of God. The future will show what human history has been able to gain from such an experience.

But this essay is concerned particularly with the Jews. It is against them that racist neo-paganism first tried its strength. Its profound desire is undoubtedly, if that be possible, to drive every Jew out of the country. But since this cannot be done, the solution has been decided upon of depriving them of political existence and of walling them up in a ghetto certainly more cruel than the ghetto of the Middle Ages, since men are now confined not because of a difference of faith and religion, against which human will and the grace of God always have recourse, but because of an irremediable difference of blood. Here we have racial anti-Semitism. To justify itself, it is not content to regard the Jews as a people, or as a race in the ethico-historical sense. They must be a race in the biological and anthropological sense of the word, and, at the same time, racism must become an ideology, a science, and a religion.

The truth is that the Jews are not a race in the biological sense of the word. We know that in man's present stage of development, there is no group of any importance, even that most favored in this respect, which is pure in race. The Jews are far from being an exception as mixtures of blood have in the course of history been as significant among them as among other human groups. Eminent scientists have concluded that in man's present historic stage, the idea of race corresponds to no anatomical-physiological reality, to no unity of "blood," but merely to types of "mentalities" produced by historic and social conditions. Its significance rests on extremely complex historical factors (of a psycho-ethico-sociological character), formed in the course of time rather than on hereditary characteristics transmitted by blood.

Not that one need deny the existence of such characteristics, nor the importance of such a science as genetics, and of such a psycho-physical basis as blood. But these biological characteristics have been strongly intermixed in the ethnic brews compounded in the course of centuries, and in any case they are only a material element absolutely unqualified to constitute by itself a criterion of human value and sufficient to rupture the rigorous unity of the human family.

Scientifically, racism seems chiefly a sort of political misappropriation of anthropology, mobilized to furnish a practical criterion of the German national community.

Philosophically and religiously speaking, it is difficult not to see in this one of the worst materialistic mockeries of man. To claim, as was done at Nuremberg in 1933, that there is "a greater gap between the lowest forms which are still called human and our superior races, than between the lowest of men and the highest of monkeys," is not simply a philosophical absurdity. It is also an insult to the Christian faith which, in affirming the spirituality and the immortality of the human soul, in preaching brotherly love for men of all races and all conditions, in teaching that Christ died for the salvation of all, affirms at the same time the natural unity of the human species, its essential distinction from other species of animals, and the equal claim of all men to the title of children of God.

It is sometimes said, and I just used the word

myself, that racism is neo-paganism: this is an insult to the pagans, who never lapsed into such brutish materialism.   The cult of so-called predestined animal blood (in reality the vehicle of original sin and all those divisions among men of which this sin is the principle) is the cult most fundamentally opposed to the Christian cult of the redeeming and vivifying blood of the Word Incarnate, by means of which all who do not reject divine grace are brought into the supernatural unity of the "race" of God and the Sons of God.

From a social and cultural viewpoint, racism degrades and humiliates to an unimaginable degree reason, thought, science and art, which are thenceforth subordinated to flesh and blood and divested of their natural "catholicity."   It brings to men, among all the modes of barbarism which threaten them today, a mode in itself the most inhuman and the most desperate of all.   For, as I have just observed, it rivets them to biological categories and fatalities from which no exercise of their freedom will enable them to escape.

II

THE DIVINE SIGNIFICANCE OF THE DISPERSION
OF ISRAEL

Let us take up the question of the dispersion of
Israel, understood in its ultimate significance.   As
I wrote in a recent study * from which I am here
borrowing several pages, whatever the economic,
political or cultural forms which cloak the problem of the dispersion of Israel among the nations,
this problem is and remains in truth a mystery,
sacred in character, of which St. Paul, in the
Epistle to the Romans, gives us the principal elements in his sublime summary.

If there are Jews among the readers of this essay,
they will understand, I am sure, that as a Christian
I try to understand something of the history of their
people from a Christian viewpoint.   They know that
according to St. Paul, we gentile Christians have
been grafted onto the predestined olive tree of Israel in place of the branches which did not recognize the Messiah foretold by the prophets.   Thus

* "L'Impossible Antisémitisme," appeared first in *Les Juifs*
(Plon, 1937), and later in our *Questions de Conscience* (Desclée
De Brouwer, 1938).

we are converts to the God of Israel who is the true God, to the Father whom Israel recognized, to the Son whom it rejected. Christianity, then, is the overflowing fulness and the supernatural realization of Judaism.

The Vocation of Israel

Referring to the Jews, his brothers in the flesh to whom he expected to be anathema, St. Paul had such a profound and tender love for them "who are Israelites, to whom belongeth the adoption as of children, and the glory, and the testament, and the giving of the law, and the service of God, and the promises: whose are the fathers, and of whom Christ came according to the flesh," * that he wrote that "if the loss of them be the reconciliation of the world, what shall the receiving of them be, but life from the dead?" † "For," continues the apostle, "I would not have you ignorant, brethren, of this mystery (lest you should be wise in your own conceits), that a blindness in part has happened in Israel, until the fulness of the Gentiles come in.

* 9 Rom. 4.   † 11 Rom. 15.

And so all Israel should be saved . . . As concerning the Gospel, indeed they are enemies for your sake: but as touching the election they are most dear for the sake of the fathers.   For the gifts and the calling of God are without repentance.   For as you also in times past did not believe God, but now have obtained mercy, through their unbelief; so these also now have not believed, for your mercy, that they also may now obtain mercy.   For God hath concluded all in unbelief, that He may have mercy on all." *

Thus from the first Israel appears to us a mystery; of the same order as the mystery of the world and the mystery of the Church.   Like them it is a mystery lying at the very core of redemption.   And we must say that, if St. Paul be right, what is called the *Jewish problem* is an *insoluble* problem, that is, one without *definitive* solution until the great reconciliation foretold by the apostle, which will resemble a resurrection from among the dead.

Between Israel and the world, as between the Church and the world, there is a suprahuman relation.   It is only by considering this triad, that one

* 11 Rom. 25, 26, 28–32.

can grasp even an enigmatic idea of the mystery of Israel.   It seems to me that we have here as our sole guiding thread a sort of inverted analogy with the Church.   We realize that the Church is not a mere administrative organization dispensing religion!   According to its own teaching about itself, it is a mysterious body in which living bonds, in order to accomplish a divine task, unite souls with one another, and with God.   The Church is the mystical body of Christ.   Indeed, Jewish thought is itself aware that in a quite different sense and in its own way, Israel is a *corpus mysticum,* a mystical body. A recent work by Erich Kahler, *Israel unter den Volkern* emphasizes this point particularly.   The bond which unifies Israel is not simply the bond of flesh and blood, or that of an ethico-historical community.   A sacred and suprahistorical bond, it is one of promise and yearning rather than of possession. In the eyes of a Christian who remembers that the promises of God are irrevocable and without repentance, Israel continues its sacred mission but in the darkness of the world, preferred, on so unforgettable an occasion, to the darkness of God.   Israel, like the Church, is in the world and not of the world. But since the day when, because its leaders chose the world, it stumbled, it is bound to the world, prisoner and victim of that world which it loves, but *of which* it is not, shall not be, and never can be. Thus is the mystery of Israel understood from a Christian viewpoint.

The communion of this mystical body is the communion of mundane hope. Israel passionately hopes, waits, yearns for the coming of God on earth, the kingdom of *God here below*. With an eternal will, a supernatural and non-rational will, it desires justice in time, in nature, and in the city of man.

So, like the world and its history, Israel and its action in the world are ambivalent realities; because the longing for the absolute in the world can take all forms, some good, others evil. Hence the fact that, in the astonishing complexity of the forms it assumes, simultaneously pregnant with good and evil, there will always be found something to glorify and something to degrade Israel. "Anti-Semites speak of Jews," said Péguy. "I am aware that I am about to speak paradoxically: the anti-Semites do not know the Jews at all." Again, he said: "I know this people well. It bears on its skin no single spot which is not painful, where there is not some old bruise, some ancient contusion, some secret woe, the memory of a secret woe, a scar, a wound, a laceration of the Orient or of the Occident."

It is not a question of deciding whether you find Jews attractive or repulsive; that is a matter of temperament.   But have they a right to common justice and the common brotherhood of man?   If men could tolerate each other only on condition of having no complaint against each other, all the provinces of every country would constantly be at war. The most curious fact, moreover, is that many anti-Semites declare that they have only praise for Jews they have known personally, but nevertheless feel hatred for the Jews as a sacred obligation.   Which is one way, among others, of paying tribute to the mystery of Israel we are considering.

But what, then, is that vocation of Israel which persists in darkness, and of which we were just speaking?   First of all, there is its vocation as a witness to the Scriptures.   But more, while the Church is assigned the labor of supernatural and supratemporal redemption of the world, Israel, we believe, is assigned, on the plane and within the limits of secular history, a task of *earthly activiza-tion* of the mass of the world.   Israel, which is not of the world, is to be found at the very heart of the world's structure, stimulating it, exasperating it, moving it.   Like an alien body, like an activating ferment injected into the mass, it gives the world no peace, it bars slumber, it teaches the world to be discontented and restless as long as the world has not God, it stimulates the movement of history.

The Spiritual Essence of Anti-Semitism

It seems to me that these considerations explain something of the spiritual essence of anti-Semitism.

The diverse specific causes which the observer may assign to anti-Semitism, all the way from the feeling of hate for the foreigner natural to any social group, down to religious hatreds — alas! that these two words may be coupled — and to the manifold inconveniences produced by some waves of immigration, mask an underlying spring of hatred deeper down.   If the world hates the Jews, it is because the world clearly senses that they will always be outsiders in a supernatural sense, it is because the world detests their passion for the absolute and the unbearable stimulus which it inflicts. It is the vocation of Israel which the world execrates.   To be hated by the world is their glory, as it is also the glory of Christians who live by faith. But Christians know that the Messiah has already conquered the world.

Thus hatred of Jews and hatred of Christians spring from a common source, from the same recalcitrance of the world, which desires to be wounded neither with the wounds of Adam nor with the wounds of the Savior, neither by the goad of Israel for its movement in time, nor by the cross of Jesus for eternal life.   We are good enough as we are, says the world, we have no need of grace or transfiguration, we ourselves will accomplish our own happiness in our own nature.   This is neither Christian hope in a helping God, nor Jewish hope for a God on earth.   It is the hope of animal life and its power, deep and, in a sense, sacred, demonic, when it masters the human being who thinks himself deceived by the emissaries of the absolute.

Racial tellurianism is anti-Semitic and anti-Christian.   Communist atheism is not anti-Semitic: it is satisfied in being against God universally.   In one as in the other, the same absolute naturalism, the same abhorrence for all asceticism and all transcendence, is to be found at work. The mystical life of the world itself aims to blossom heroically, as it were; every mystical body constituted apart from the world must be rejected as such.

The French are not inclined to prostrate themselves before the earth; even when they lose their heads, it is in order to worship the goddess of Reason. That is why it seems to me that they will never be deeply anti-Semitic. They make fun of Jews as they do of "les curés," but among them genuine anti-Semitic mania never goes beyond the limits of a glorified petty bourgeois ideology. I do not overlook the violent propaganda being spread today in certain circles, I think artificially and sometimes venally. Those who know the French youth well, particularly the French Catholic youth, are confident that it will never march except in the name of liberty, generosity and intelligence.

Jews and Christians

Have I succeeded in giving some idea of the pathos of the situation of the Jewish people? In explaining how, often despite itself, and while manifesting, sometimes in contrasting forms, a materialistic messianism which is the dark face of its vocation to the absolute, but manifesting also admirable ardor, intelligence and dynamism, the Jewish people bears witness to the divine in human history? Thence come the conflicts and the tension which, under all sorts of masks, necessarily prevail between Israel and the nations.

It is an illusion to believe that such tension can completely vanish. To desire to put an end to the problem by anti-Semitic violence, openly persecutory or politically mitigated, is villainy, one of those villainies natural to the human animal (whether he be an Arab and himself the descendant of Shem, or a Slav, a Latin or a German), and from which only Christianity, to the extent that it is really lived, can deliver the nations. The sole road is to accept the state of tension and to face it in each specific case, not with hatred, but with that concrete intelligence which love demands from each, so that one may come to an early understanding with one's adversary while traveling together, and in the consciousness that "all have sinned and need the glory of God," *omnes quidem peccaverunt, et egent gloria Dei.* "The history of the Jews," said Léon Bloy, "thwarts the history of the human race as a dike thwarts the flood, to raise its level."

On the spiritual plane, the drama of love between Israel and its God, if we are to believe St. Paul, will reach a dénouement only with the reconciliation of the Synagogue and the Church. If there is to be no earlier truly definitive solution to the problem of Israel, there are nevertheless some partial or provisional solutions, specific responses whose discovery is the task of political wisdom and which each historic age must seek.

The historic age in which we live is a period of accumulated difficulties for the Jewish people. In the economic field the renunciation of free competition, the rise of autarchical and state capitalist régimes, deal a body blow to Jewish economic pursuits. Recently published studies of the economic situation of world Jewry indicate the growing pauperization of the Jewish masses.

In the political and moral fields, the development of various types of totalitarianism, all of which regard the non-conformist as a biological

enemy of the secular community, menaces the natural attachment of the Jews to independence and
liberty.

In the spiritual field, the upsurge of unprece-
dentedly ferocious forms of paganism signifies an
inevitable conflict, already terribly begun, with that
people who, surrounded by the pagans of another
age, knew how to pay heroic tribute to the sanctity
of the personal and transcendent God.

I have come to believe that if the world should
triumph over the errors and evils oppressing it today and should contrive to establish the rule of a
civilization, new and more consonant with human
dignity, the solutions at once pluralist and person-
alist which would have to prevail generally in such
a régime, will likewise characterize those efforts to
regulate the Jewish question which such an historic
climate must inspire.   As I tried to explain elsewhere,* a pluralism founded on the dignity of the
human person, and established on the basis of complete equality of civic rights, and effective respect
for the liberties of the person in his individual and

* Cf. "L'Impossible Antisémitisme," in *Questions de Conscience*,
Paris, 1938, pages 86–89.

social life, would then recognize in certain determined matters, an ethico-juridical status proper to
various spiritual families, or even, sometimes, to
various national communities which enter into the
convivium of the temporal city. But such solutions,
which though far removed from the old Liberalism,
are thoroughly opposed to the ignominious medie-
valist Hitlerian parody, and which tend to strengthen
the bonds of justice and brotherly friendship between the various elements of the same civil society,
could only be considered in a general new régime of
civilization, freed from the ills of capitalistic materialism as well as from the even greater ills of
Fascism, Racism and Communism. Those who at
present suggest a special status for the Jews are
actually thinking of measures of discrimination
against them. They are the victims of the absurd
illusion, according to which the Jewish question,
poisoned as are all the questions of today by the
general crisis suffered by a civilization which is
sick and in a state of transformation, is the only or
the principal cause of this crisis; they imagine that
the "solution" which consists of sacrificing the Jews
would end the evils whose roots plunge, in fact, into

the very depths of the economic, moral, spiritual and political structures of our civilization. Infected by the contagion of the errors propagated by the racist mentality, they serve this mentality, whether they wish to or not. Some of them are fierce anti-Semites who pretend to be good apostles. Others protest that they are not anti-Semites, and consider themselves as dispassionate *realists:* they are Mr. Hitler's messengers, who have *not even* the excuse of passion.

Strictly speaking, the only suitable "realism" here would be the one which understands the reality of the horror whereby the cult of hatred and the rejection of all human sentiment threaten the universe; the only realism which a Christian has the right to profess in such a matter is the one that warns us that the least word which might convey the merest shadow of an indulgence or concession toward racism, runs the risk of bearing an ugly complicity, and of dripping with innocent blood.

If we now turn more particularly toward the Christians, it appears, that being themselves grafted onto the olive tree of Israel, they must look on the men involved in the Jewish tragedy with a brotherly eye and, as the apostle Paul teaches them, not without trembling for themselves. It is certainly possible for Christians to be anti-Semites, since one observes the phenomenon frequently enough. But it is possible for them only when they obey the spirit of the world rather than the spirit of Christianity.

Strangely enough certain Christians are heard to remark: "Has the world been moved (they say) by the massacres of so many Christians in Russia, Spain, and Mexico? We will be stirred by the Jewish persecutions when the world will be stirred by the sufferings of our own."

When I hear this manner of reasoning, I wonder how it is that from one day to the next, and without even telling me anything about it, my religion has been changed. Does the Gospel teach that if a brother has sinned against me, by omission or otherwise, it is justifiable to sin against him in the same fashion? Jesus said: "These things you ought to have done, and not to leave those undone." Now it is said: "Because these things have been left undone, you ought not to do those." Because certain people have been lacking in justice and in love, others must be similarly deficient. . .

It is not exact to say that the world remained indifferent to the suffering of Christians in Russia, Spain and Mexico.* It is, however, exact that many who today are full of indignation because of Racism remained quite cold regarding the discriminatory laws enacted by certain governments against religious Orders, and regarding the anti-Christian persecutions which have raged or are raging in so many countries. I object to such unjust indifference and such one-eyed pity. But I do not want to lay myself open to the same objection.

Among careless or partisan writers many historic confusions arise from the fact of the commingling in medieval civilization of the affairs of the Church and the affairs of a secular commonwealth religiously organized, where mundane interests and both the good and evil of human social life were steeped in religion. If one makes the proper dis-

---

* Notably, various rabbinical organizations in the United States and France protested against the persecutions of Christians, as was revealed in a news release of the *Catholic Worker*, December 5, 1938.

tinctions, one can see that, in a temporal civilization where the régime of the ghetto — not to speak
of the drama of the Marranos and the Spanish In-
quisition — lent itself to the worst anti-Semitic passions and excesses, the Church itself and as such,
was not responsible for the excesses, even if some
of its ministers were.* It is well enough known
that the Popes repeatedly defended the Jews, notably against the absurd charge of ritual murder, and
that all in all the Jews were generally less unhappy
and less badly treated in the Papal States than elsewhere.

Western civilization, emerging from the Holy
Roman Empire and the medieval régime, while in
jeopardy of collapsing in other respects, as we
know, freed itself from the strong impurities which
this régime entailed. And it would be a singular
aberration if Christians wished to return to those
impurities at the moment when they have lost their

---

* If a unilateral selection of texts were not made, and if there
were sufficient acquaintance with the philosophy of history, it
would be understood that neither the policy adopted at certain
periods regarding the Jews by medieval Christendom, nor the
supervening mistakes and abuses which may have happened, prove
that the Catholic Church is bound to anti-Semitism. I mention this
for the benefit of certain Italian Fascist writers, as well as for
certain American anti-Fascist writers. . .

historic reason for existing.   Today anti-Semitism
is no longer one of those accidental blemishes of a
secular Christendom in which evil was mixed
with the good.   It contaminates Christians like an
error of the spirit.   I recall to the reader's mind
that in a document of the Holy Office dated September 5, 1928, which was directed against the mistakes of a too zealous "Association of the Friends
of Israel," the Catholic Church has explicitly condemned this error of anti-Semitism.   Racist errors
were again condemned, April 13, 1938, in a pon-
tifical document (letter of the Sacred Congregation
of Seminaries and Universities).

It is well known that Pope Pius XI spoke out
vigorously against the racist campaign and racist
measures inaugurated by the Italian government
in imitation of the German government.   To the
concept and word *race*, figuring in the theories imported from Germany, he opposed magnificently
the ancient Latin idea of *gens* and *populus*, the con-
notation of which belong much more to the moral
than to the biological order.

The following passages of a discourse pronounced
in September 1938, before the directors of the Bel-

gian Catholic Radio Agency, are also to be noted. Commenting upon the words of the Canon of the Mass *sacrificium Patriarchae nostri Abrahae,* the sacrifice of our father Abraham, the Pope said, "Notice that Abraham is called our Patriarch, our ancestor. Anti-Semitism is incompatible with the thought and sublime reality expressed in this text. It is a movement in which we Christians can have no part whatsoever. . . Anti-Semitism is unacceptable. Spiritually we are Semites."

Spiritually we are Semites. No stronger word has been spoken by a Christian against anti-Semitism, and this Christian is the successor of the apostle Peter.

As for its moral characterization from the Catholic viewpoint, anti-Semitism, if it spreads among those calling themselves disciples of Jesus Christ, seems to be a pathological phenomenon which indicates a deterioration of Christian conscience when it becomes incapable of accepting its own historic responsibilities and of remaining existentially faithful to the high exigencies of Christian truth. Then, instead of recognizing the trials and shocks of history as the visitations of God, and instead of assuming those burdens of justice and charity demanded by that fact, it turns aside to substitute phantoms relating to an entire race, phantoms which derive a certain consistency from various real or fancied pretexts. And in giving free rein to feelings of hate which it believes justified by religion, it seeks for itself a sort of alibi.

It is no little matter, however, for a Christian to hate or to despise or to wish to treat degradingly the race from which sprung his God and the Immaculate Mother of his God. That is why the bitter zeal of anti-Semitism always turns in the end into a bitter zeal against Christianity itself.

"Imagine," wrote Léon Bloy, "that people about you were to speak continually of your father and your mother with the greatest contempt, and to have for them only insults or outrageous sarcasm. What would be your sentiments? Well, that is exactly what is happening to Our Lord Jesus Christ. We forget, or rather we do not wish to know, that as a man Our Lord was a Jew, the epitomé par excellence of the Jewish nature, the Lion of Judah; that His Mother was a Jewess, the flower of the Jewish race; that the apostles were Jews, along with all the prophets; finally, that our whole liturgy is based on Jewish books. How, then, express the enormity of the outrage and the blasphemy involved in vilifying the Jewish race?"

III

THE PRESENT TRAGEDY OF THE JEWISH PEOPLE

Everybody knows that the Jews miss no opportunity for lamentation. If they so well understand weeping, it is because they have a sempiternal habit of sorrowing and because they are disarmed. To-day, in any case, it may be said that, when it comes to persecutions, they are plentifully supplied.

The third part of this essay, in which I shall speak of matters of fact concerning the actual situation of the Jews in various countries, will obviously be but a brief summary. If one were to enumerate in detail all the types of oppression involved, one could never conclude.

Before examining briefly the effects of anti-

Semitism in Germany, Rumania and Poland, let us say a few words about the situation of the Jews in Russia.

The Jews in Russia

Perhaps some people will be surprised: does not the U.S.S.R. make a boast, and justifiably, of having officially proscribed anti-Semitism? Has it not given the Jews, as it has members of other ethnic groups, equality in law and free access to schools and universities? Yes, that is true. Nevertheless, Russia is one of the countries of the world in which Israel is most threatened.

I do not here speak simply of the economic ruin which the Soviet régime brought on the Jewish masses. Ninety percent of the Jews of Russia lived from trade, industry and crafts. Their means of livelihood have been harder hit than those of the peasant masses, because the new régime no longer tolerates merchants or independent craftsmen. For them, the economic disaster is thoroughgoing.

No, what I want to point out above all is that, if *the Jews* can live, however miserably, in Russia, *Jewry* and *Judaism* are condemned to death. Their assimilation, forced assimilation, is succeeding only *too well*.

The struggle has not been and is not being carried on against the Jewish race, but against the Jewish religion, as against all religions. Violent persecution, conducted by atheistic Jews, has burst on religious Jews. "Here," one Jewish author writes, "it is the Jew who is the Jew's worst enemy." Finally, the great mass of Jewish youth is cut off from religion. Only the older generation perseveres, but "in the face of the hostility of the governing classes, it dare not move, and religion is doomed."

"In this country," writes the same author, "where the Jews twenty years ago were still the most solid bulwark of Judaism, the Jewish religion is about to be destroyed." *

And, by the same token, Jewish culture is doomed. Rabbinical schools and almost all synagogues are closed. Teaching in the Hebrew tongue, folkways, religious holidays, circumcision, the rites of the Mosaic code, all are practically forbidden. A

---

* Arthur Ruppin, *The Jews in the Modern World*, New York, 1934.

mighty state pressure works, on the other hand, in favor of mixed marriages, with the result that the Jewish ethnic and cultural entity is rapidly vanishing.* Likewise, Zionism, regarded as an "imperialist" movement, is rigorously repressed, and every attempt at Zionist propaganda becomes the object of immediate arrest and exile.†

It was recently said of Yiddish literature that its force and originality "come from *its impotence not to be* religious." ‡   In a general sense, there is no Jewish people without the God of the Scriptures, if His presence be only in the dead bones of a tradition devoid of faith, such as Zionism, at least, respects and collects.

It is a remarkably significant phenomenon and one which confirms our earlier reflections, that everything proceeds as though a profound hatred of the Scriptures, wherein God testifies to Himself, rebounds on Israel itself as a mystical body, and Israel, the mystical body, is never afflicted but Israel, the people, feels the same blow.

* In the Jewish state — that is to say, in the region populated by Jews — which the Soviets have tried to create in Birobidjan, specifically Jewish culture is not in the best of shape.

† Olav Leroi, *La Croix*, January 30–31, 1938.

‡ Paul Fierens, *Revue des poètes catholiques*, no. 1, 1937.

The Jews in Germany

We have dealt with German racism chiefly from the viewpoint of principles. Is it really necessary to recall now how it works out in practice?

According to the law of April 7, 1933 (that with the famous *Aryan clause*), supplemented by other legislative acts of the same year, all non-Aryans, that is to say, all human beings who bear in their veins 100 percent or 50 percent or — when they have had a single Jewish grandfather or grandmother — 25 percent of Jewish blood, are barred from public posts as well as, directly or indirectly and by means of provocations, from the liberal and "cultural" professions.

Jews have been forbidden to participate in the world of the theatre, the press, literature, music destined for the Aryan masses, or to become teachers or students in German universities. They are the objects of special laws, not to unite them to the life of the commonwealth, but to segregate them as an inferior and noxious race.* Let them work out a

* It is notable that the Jews form but a small proportion of the German population. Before Hitler came to power, there were in Germany about 550,000 Jews. From 1933 to the end of 1937, according to the careful statistical studies of Dr. Kurt Zielenziger of

ghetto culture?   Even if they were to be encouraged to do so, it would be as slaves are encouraged to sing their songs to themselves before death comes. Let them be economically productive?   Even if some of them may hold important positions, in many sectors of economic life they are dispossessed for the benefit of Aryans.   Jewish shops are boycotted. Aryans guilty of buying from Jewish merchants are threatened and molested.   Jewish origin becomes a valid reason for the discharge of any employee.

Blood dominates everything, dominates intelligence and good will, grace, and baptism.   The children of a baptized Jew must be taught in a Jewish, not in a Christian school.

We know that in September, 1935, the Nuremberg laws, those "laws for the protection of German blood and honor," deprived the Jews of the title of citizen and of political rights.   We know that the same laws forbid marriage (as well as extra-marital sexual relations) between Jews and non-Jews under penalty of prison and hard labor.*   These punishments hav-

---

Amsterdam, published in the review *Population*, about 135,000 Jews left Germany.   Some 30,000 went to other European countries, the rest to Palestine, South America, the United States and South Africa.

* See page 49.

ing proven insufficiently efficacious, some anti-Semites propose now to institute capital punishment for the crime of what they call *race shame* or *racial pollution*.

Let us cite here, as an example, certain facts which were collected by Louis Roubaud, a French journalist endowed with great objectivity, during an inquiry recently made by him in Germany, and which he published in the *Petit Parisien* (March, 1939):

Posters warn imprudent citizens: "Every girl so forgetful of her race as to visit a Jew or to receive him in her house, or to go for a walk with him, will be shaved and exposed in the public square. We invite the Germans conscious of their dignity to watch over Christian women who cultivate a Jew, to give us their addresses, and to inform us of their behaviour."

Such punitive exhibitions are a current spectacle for citizens of large and small towns.

I passed but one day in Nuremberg, Emil told me . . . the inhabitants did not look surprised! they did not react. I was coming out of my hotel, when the procession passed before me. . . I first beheld six soldiers in arms, pushing in front of them a young boy in women's clothes . . . it was not a boy, but a girl, completely bald, and yet pretty, with blue eyes bright with tears, and so thin and fragile! After having shaved her head, the soldiers had hung round her neck a sign: "I HAVE GIVEN MYSELF TO A JEW." She was exhausted, stumbling. Having arrived before the hotel, she let herself fall on the greasy pavement, pretending to have fainted. They kicked her to make her get up, and one of the kicks marked her delicate face with blood and mud. . . I had the courage to join the loiterers who were following. When she was really unable to walk any more, the soldiers lifted her on their shoulders to show her to the distant spectators. . .

The Fritsche trial is not an exceptional case. M. Fritsche, a widower of 45, is the father of a boy of 18, a "boy in uniform," like many others, and who is undergoing training in a camp with others. M. Fritsche, sober, fond of sport, is not an old man. Sarah was his wife's friend. She is 35 and pretty. The honest affection which he felt for her before becoming a widower, transformed itself into love. He commits the "crime." And immediately, the "accomplices" are frightened, they try to cross the French frontier. His "son in uniform" denounces him, bears testimony against him during the trial. Fifteen months of hard labour.

A sentence of the Tribunal of the Empire dated January 18, 1938, condemns to ten months of hard labour, young F . . . , who is not a Jew, but who thought that he was one, when he committed the crime of letting himself be seduced by a fair German. This young man, who was legally the posthumous son of a Jew, married to a Christian, learnt during the trial that his mother, long before his birth, was the mistress of a pure Aryan, Dr. G. . . "Your father was for more than a year in the hospital, where he was to die," the mother tearfully told him. "I only saw him once a week in a common ward. My affair with Dr. G . . . dates from that time."

The accused asks for his mother's and Dr. G's testimony.
But according to jurisprudence, the intention suffices for
the crime of "rassenchande" (race shame) to be committed.
Not even the intention! . . . The simple appearances, a
beginning of presumption! . . . If the Jew is at the same
time a former social-democrat, the police enters arbitrarily
the undesirable into the category of "rassenchande."

Thus, M. Samter, a Hindenburg (Upper Silesia) merchant, before the suppression of Jewish shops. He ought
to be careful with that lady-client who, notwithstanding
the bill "Jude" in evidence in the shop-window, did not
hesitate to bargain over a radio-set. This happened in
the evening, just before the closing of the shop. And
Samter was alone! He should have found out about the
lady's religion. She was a Miss Martha Waldbrun, who
made him test several radio-sets, not being able to make
up her mind, leaning over the merchant's shoulder, under
the excuse to make him explain a detail. . . The police-
man arrived. . . During the trial, Miss Waldbrun, seized
with remorse, admits that she had been paid by the police.
Samter, entirely absorbed by the sale of the set, did not
make a single gesture, had not the slightest thought tinged
with gallantry. . . Notwithstanding this fact, he is ruth-
lessly condemned to *six years* of hard labour. Horrified
by the consequence of her act, Miss Waldbrun commits
suicide. "She did not want to survive her blemish," the
newspapers declare.

One could cite endless facts. . . Not only must the Jews
not run the risk of giving life outside their race, they are
also forbidden to save life. Before committing suicide,
the famous specialist of children's diseases, Professor

Knoepfelmacher of Vienna, wrote the following words: "I have saved the lives of 60,000 children; today, I am obliged to take my own life."

. . . This sectarianism does not only concern the doctor, it also forbids medecines of Jewish origin, even those whose benefits have been long known all over the world.

Serotherapy, which saves thousands of children from diphtheria, was introduced in Germany by Von Behrend. Let German babies die rather than be healed by a Jew! In two years the number of child victims of croup has risen from 3992 in 1932 to 6372 in 1934. . . The parents of the tiny creature condemned to die, implore the Christian doctor to inject the salutary serum . . . the doctor trembles, for he remembers the terrible condemnation pronounced by Streicher: "Serotherapy represents the specifically Jewish idea of soiling German blood with the blood of animals different from the human race."

The imagination can picture but a small part of what these manifold legal provisions, with the accompanying illegal excesses — ignoble parades of wretched men carrying mocking placards, Jewish cemeteries profaned by the hundreds, violence and humiliations of all sorts, confiscations of property, denunciations and travesties of justice — produce in the way of suffering and anguish, misery and dishonor for unfortunate human beings.   Naturally, suicide thrives.   The labor of teachers and propa-

gandists poisons the hearts of the common people, of
children, of the poor, with hate and contempt for
Jews and other victims of persecution.   But wait!
Worst of all is the degradation of human dignity
among the persecuted.   Not alone are there in some
Berlin public squares yellow benches reserved for
Jews.   The worst is the fact that one may see Jews,
sad weary Jews, sitting on these benches.   And there
have been families of a Jewish father and an Aryan
mother in which children have extracted from the
mother a confession of adultery in order to prove
that they were born of pure Aryan blood and had a
right to civic life.

But is there ever an end to lust and cruelty?
These augment *ad infinitum*.   New means of oppression are invented each day.   Even the name of
Jehovah has been proscribed.   The racist persecution in the course of the year 1938 has produced
spectacles which show that it is always possible to
dishonor human nature *still further*.*

I know that Germany and racism are not necessarily identified and although such matters "go without saying," I must nevertheless note here that hate

* See pages 69 *et seq.*

for a whole people would be a great madness, and that despite racism and the anti-Christianity which are ravaging German hearts, the human reserves of Germanic culture are not exhausted.   But if the moral cataclysms sweeping a country cannot prevent those who hope to secure thereby the peace of the world from desiring international agreements, those same desires, in turn, do not prevent the truth from being uttered.   The example of German anti-Semitism, which the National Socialist leaders conjured up and continue violently to provoke, and which they simultaneously are trying to regularize, while welding it into a favored instrument of foreign influence, the example of this anti-Semitism and its propaganda which is being furthered everywhere, in America as in Europe, is a bad omen for such civilization as remains to us.   Italy, for political reasons, has begun to cultivate anti-Semitic sentiments, a novelty for her.   Since the summer of 1938, Italian Fascism has become deliberately racist (I will return to this matter in a further section). Under moral and cultural forms, without overt brutality or legislative trappings, there was rather severe anti-Semitism in Austria before the *Anschluss*.

Now the native country of the child Mozart is no more. The new events which in recent months have changed the face of Central Europe, and to which I shall refer later, have been accompanied in these lands by a general and implacable surge of anti-Semitism.

Previously, other countries were already affected, Poland, of which I shall speak shortly, and also, to a lesser degree, Lithuania, and Yugoslavia. Anti-Semitic propaganda, supported by Germany, is attempting to trouble many countries in South America.

In Rumania a wave of terror broke forth in the beginning of the year 1938.

The Jews in Rumania

The Jews of Rumania have long been treated as legal inferiors. Despite the promises made at the Congress of Berlin in 1878, it was only with the Treaty of 1919, following the World War, and with the Constitution of the enlarged Rumanian state, that the equality of all Rumanian citizens before the law, "without distinction of race, language or religion," was proclaimed. In annexing Bessarabia, Bukowina, Transylvania, the Banat and Maramuresh, with some 9,000,000 inhabitants, Rumania undertook, in accord with a quite obvious rule of international public law, to recognize as entitled to the benefits of Rumanian law all the Jews, some 600,000, living in those territories.

I have but limited confidence in statistics, particularly the demographic statistics of countries subject to nationality conflicts and disputes.   Relying, however, on the official data of the Rumanian statistical bureau, and rounding off figures upward rather than downward, it would seem reasonable to draw the following conclusions.   Old Rumania counted some 250,000 Jews, long assimilated.   Adding this figure to that which I just gave for the territories newly annexed, we see that before the war there were 850,000 Jews in the present domain of the kingdom of Rumania.   Today there are a few more or less, less rather than more,* that is, about four and one half percent of the total population.   Of

* According to the figures of the Bucharest Demographic Institute, the figure would be 760,000 to 765,000. Of these some 30,000 have, since 1920, been refused naturalization; these have only duties, and no rights as Rumanian subjects. Their number is augmented by some thousands of others, whom the liberal cabinet of Mr. Tataresco, which preceded the anti-Semitic government of Mr. Goga, deprived arbitrarily of their Rumanian citizenship.

this number, it is estimated that some 10,000 are Jews who fled from Russia since the war and settled in Rumania "fraudulently." [1]

Nevertheless, in January and February 1938 the officials in power announced the intention of withdrawing Rumanian nationality and the right of settlement and residence in the kingdom, from 500,000 Jews, accused by Mr. Goga of having entered the country by fraud, although King Carol would reckon the number at half this figure. The cry of reprobation was being raised not against 10,000 Jews, but against 500,000.

Thus, even for the best statistical sleight-of-hand artists, it was difficult to reconcile this project with the solemn obligation of the treaty of December 9, 1919. Moreover, for what purpose? The truth is that racism, of which the pledges of treaties mean very little, has sown a whirlwind in Rumania, and wanted to settle in the most rapid and brutal way not only with 10,000 or 250,000 or 500,000 Jews, but with the entire Jewish population of the country.

[1] After the establishment of Nazism in Germany, a great number of German Jewish families *crossed* Rumania, which admitted them only in transit. Very few remained. The proportion of German Jews settled in the country since 1933 is insignificant.

All Jewish citizens were barred from public posts. It was decided to close to Jews certain professions and businesses, to expropriate their agricultural enterprises, to exclude them from the theatre and motion pictures, to take away from a large number of Jewish doctors, engineers, architects and lawyers, the right to practice their professions.   It did not matter that the country districts suffered from a terrible shortage of doctors.   The Jewish doctors must first be crushed.   The Iron Guard organized a terror against Jewish students in the professional schools and against Jewish attorneys.   The Blueshirts inspired hatred against the Jews among the rural masses, hounded Jewish peasants by the hundreds, compelled them to flee wretchedly from their farms.   And all this seemed a beginning only.   The worst threats, a mortal terror, hung over hundreds of thousands of human beings for several weeks.

"Well," Mr. Octavian Goga told the Tharaud brothers, "couldn't we send them far away . . . somewhere . . . to some island which they could never leave? . . . Warships of all countries could cruise around it. . ." (The Goga government was short-lived.   It fell quickly; and not long afterwards, the newspapers announced the death of Mr. Goga himself.)

It seems that in Rumania, Church and State collaborated in this new style of government, if one may rely on the declarations of the late Patriarch of the Orthodox Rumanian Church, Miron Cristea, published in a Bucharest newspaper.* There he expressed the opinion that Jews had "bled white" the Rumanian people, and would soon force the Rumanians to "abandon their homes and their hearths and wander through the world," and that there must be somewhere on the face of the globe, "in Africa, in Australia, in Asia, in the islands," some free land to which the Jews could be relegated. "I do not know enough about world geography to tell you where this country is," added this minister of the Gospel. He was to succeed Mr. Goga at the head of the Rumanian government, and was obliged by political necessities to renounce that useful geographical inquiry, as well as the legal realization of his feelings.

Let us recall the declaration adopted in 1931 by the Catholic Union of International Studies: "The

* *Curentul,* August 19, 1937.

members of a national group (that is, of a minority) are bound to all those duties and obligations toward the state in which they are subjects, that Christian morality and politics impose on the conscience of citizens.   They enjoy all the rights which both accredit to man and to the citizen." Monseigneur Beaupin recently wrote: "To reaffirm such principles, applicable to all lands and to all times, is not to intervene in the internal politics of any particular State."   Moreover, Rumania had the wisdom to reject the racist madness of the Goga government. The Iron Guard, whose plots, inspired by Nazism, were threatening the Crown, was dissolved; and severe judiciary sanctions were taken against its leader, who was later killed, according to the police report, while trying to escape from prison.   The anti-Semitic mood remains very strong in this country, but the projects of legal persecution were abandoned.

The Jews in Poland

In Germany anti-Semitism has taken an anti-Christian form; in Rumania it has taken an Orthodox form, strongly tinged with anti-Catholicism: at the Congress of the "Orthodox Brotherhood" held in November, 1937, speakers put Catholicism on a plane with Communism; the Congress demanded the denunciation of the Papal Concordat, and denounced the Vatican's "aggressive and denationalizing proselytism." Rumanian Catholics complain of being the object of calumnies and of campaigns of hatred which lead to religious war.

In Poland, although the heads of the Catholic Church, notably Cardinal Hlond, have repudiated "systematic and unconditional hostility toward the Jews," anti-Semitism has taken a Catholic form, from the fact that, sociologically, it is natural, all too natural, that passions, however misleading, which claim to defend a country's national interests, should claim also support from its traditional religion.

I am aware that in general Poland has rejected the doctrine of pagan racism and that its government would like to limit the conflict to the economic field. I am aware that there are in Poland three to three and one-half million Jews, a little more than ten percent of the total population, so that the problems which I discussed at the beginning of this essay and which concern countries with a large Jewish national minority, are more real for Poland than for any other country.   Nevertheless, it remains a fact that intense anti-Semitism persists there, further stimulated by German influence and by the bad national economic situation.   By exalting, on the one hand, shadowy national susceptibilities, and, on the other, aggravated sufferings and claims, this anti-Semitism risks leading to quite insoluble difficulties.   In recent years, particularly in 1937, the Polish Jews have suffered a persecution which, although not legally organized as in Germany, nevertheless tends to render life entirely impossible for them.

I hastily record — alas, it is always that same litany — the extensive boycott of Jewish merchants and artisans (what is called "dry" anti-Semitism) [1] the frightful multiplication of brawls, pillagings,

[1] Those who preach this mass boycott as an economic remedy for the atrophy of non-Jewish trade, forget that, however desirable it may be to replace the régime of free competition by one of organized communal labor, the operation of any given régime cannot be violently disturbed.   In fact, the boycott in question is part of a scheme to reduce Jewish traders and artisans to famine, in order to force them to emigrate.   (As though the Jews, especially those of Poland, were not predisposed to furnish a great quota of emigrants, *if only they could!*   If only other countries would open their frontiers!)   Such a boycott adds a spice of cruelty to a situation already deplorable enough for all.   And what it certainly contrives to do, is to develop evil passions without restraint.

pogroms with casualties of dead and wounded, systematic travesties of justice, a tragic increase in violence, blind popular hatreds. By setting upon the
Jews, peasants dying of hunger are induced to believe that they will thus find a solution to the agrarian
question and to rural pauperism. A just redistribu-
tion of land, such as other States effected in order
to head off worse developments, is just what the
great landowners wish to avoid at any price, and
that is why they strive to turn the anger of the poor
against the Jews. The most odious events are those
which occur in circles that, presumably reserved to
science and culture, transform themselves into the
vehicles of racist influence, and provokers of passions. In January 1937, there were university troubles on which I prefer, for the sake of the good
name of the students of Warsaw, not to dwell at
length. We know that recently, giving in to anti-
Semitic pressure, the Polish university authorities
have installed separate benches for Jewish students,
thus creating ghettos in classrooms. Numerous Polish professors have protested against this measure,
and some of them — like those Jewish students who,
rather than sit on such benches, stand during lec-

tures — have also insisted on lecturing on their feet.

I must add — I will not hide an aspect of the matter which pains me — that for sociological reasons to which I just alluded, it is generally the Catholic sections of the Polish population which seem most touched with anti-Semitism. Deplorable incitements have spread among them, and the Catholic press has all too often been an accomplice. Often, too, there seems to be a spirit which, without endorsing excesses committed against Jews, resigns itself, and, without professing anti-Semitism, regards the Jewish drama with the indifference of the *reasonable* man who goes coldly along his way. But he is our fellow-creature, this wounded Jew lying half dead on the road from Jerusalem to Jericho. . .

And as for those believers who think they are serving Christianity by binding its cause to that of political, and violent, and unjust parties, we know that in reality they profoundly damage the cause they would serve.

To close this section, let me recall that, according to the treaty of June 29, 1919, the Polish government is obligated to "accord to all inhabitants full and entire protection of life and liberty, without distinction as to birth, nationality, race or religion." Article VII specifies that "all Polish nationals shall be equal before the law and shall enjoy identical civil and political rights, without distinction of race, language or religion; differences in religion, creed or belief shall not be grounds for depriving any Polish national of his enjoyment of any civil or political rights, notably admission to public employment, offices or honors, or the exercise of the various professions and industries."   This, we must grant, goes rather badly with the *numerus clausus*, ghetto benches and the indulgence, not to say worse, too often extended to pogromists by judicial authorities.*

1938–1939

In the course of the year 1938 the situation of the Jews throughout the world became still worse.

I will mention first the troubles and massacres in Palestine.   The short-range policy, so long hesitant

* On the question of the Jewish drama in Poland, it will be useful to consult the well-documented articles of Oscar de Ferenzy in *Juste Parole*, 1937 and 1938.

and weak, of the mandate power bears heavy responsibilities.   More fundamentally, it may be that
the ancient rivalry of Ismael and Israel demands,
for its appeasement, a fraternal generosity of which
neither have shown themselves capable since the
establishment of the Zionist home. Nor am I unaware
that this establishment was inevitably subject to the
capitalistic and colonial methods by which all great
temporal realizations of this kind are impregnated
in the world of today.   On the other hand, the Jews,
who have shown admirable self-restraint (in spite
of the theories of some extremists who wanted to
answer terrorism with terrorism), are growing ex-
asperated by three years of murder, lawlessness and
complete governmental inefficiency; and a few ter-
roristic acts may have been committed on their part,
though these are the exception.   It remains, that
the rights acquired by the heroic labor of the Jewish
pioneers, as well as the rights granted to them after
the war by international agreements, are unques-
tionable.   The Jews in Palestine are suffering unjust violence, and there as elsewhere, sympathy must
go first to the victims and not to the aggressors.

If persecution has subsided in Rumania, — at

least regarding discriminatory laws and violence
that the pro-German elements had been willing to
provoke — on the other hand, Fascist Italy has
avowedly adopted racism in theory and practice.
What reasons can be assigned to this surprising
wave of official anti-Semitism in a country where
the Jewish population is very small, has been established for centuries, and is remarkably assimilated?
Must one not ascribe it to the weakness of the ideo-
logical and dynamic power whereby Fascism is necessarily dragged along by the élan of its rival and
ally, National-Socialist totalitarianism? Is it not
reduced to imitating ostentatiously (while pro-
claiming that it owes nothing to anyone) the Hitlerian pseudo-mysticism of race and blood? Must
one not think that anti-Semitism is for the Fascist
chiefs merely a way of preparing a general policy
which — naturally in the name of Latin and Christian civilization — will place the sword of the
Prophet and Mussulman passions in the hands of
Il Duce? The fact is, in any event, that those who
have, as we do, a reverence for Italian soil penetrated with humanity and civilization, and who know
all that the world and culture owe to the thinkers

and artists of this admirable country, and to the
virtues of its people, feel a profound sorrow and a
sort of shame in seeing its present masters striving
thus to debase its history.   The most vexatious
measures have begun to be taken in Italy against
the Jews, thrown out of the positions they occupied
in governmental and cultural activities, and driven
on a large scale out of economic activities.   There
too, as in Austria, one saw men who had devoted
their lives to spiritual culture and to the progress of
science, and to whom the very right of existence was
now denied, answer this barbarous negation by
suicide.   A legislative proposal, aimed at prevent-
ing the marriage of Jews and non-Jews, gave rise to
a protest on the part of the Catholic Church, which
declared it contrary to the concordat between it and
the Italian State.   If the Fascist legislators hesitate
before this protest and attenuate the juridical dis-
positions they had at first in mind, they will not give
up, however, the intention of practically attaining
their aim through diverted means.   The great majority of the Italian population is disgusted with
this imported anti-Semitism; but the leaders of the

régime assert their firm determination to impose it by force and to aggravate it.

But it is in Germany that the spectacle is most tragic. Everyone recollects the events echoed in the press of the world; what the public knows less well, however, is the depths of wickedness and contempt for the human person reached on the one side, and the sorrow and agony reached on the other. The annexation of Austria provoked an unprecedented wave of violence, and unbelievable scenes of sadistic cruelty. Measures of ruthless persecution condemn the Jews to slow death, and to despair. Persecutors were seen rejoicing at the suicides to which their ferocious actions led a great number of unfortunates — is this not a good method of racial selection? And who will tell of the ignominious treatment suffered in concentration camps by so many victims — Jews, Catholics and political suspects? The Catholic religion is, moreover, more and more seriously threatened, and the world can witness the inglorious collapse of the system of an Austrian State religion inherited from Josephism. Such Austrians as were blinded by the desire for power and who imagined that because they were more intelligent they could tame Nazism and politically profit by it, opposing at the same time its anti-religious excesses, are now dreadfully disappointed. Even the Austrian Nazis are disappointed. Besides, it may be that the Austrian temperament, with its sensitiveness and its fantasy and its suppleness, apparently passive but which employs all the methods of discipline, will provoke many an internal difficulty in the immense Prussian machinery which now holds it in its grip. Alas, Europeans still remember all that Austria represented for their civilization; they remember the mission which was Austria's, to improve the gifts of the Germanic mind in the direction of happiness and freedom, not of barbarism. The collapse of this country and its absorption by the German Reich, following the errors accumulated by the victors of the war of 1914–1918, and the retaliation that the vanquished demanded from the dark forces evoked by a political sorcery which surprised the universe, are the most sinister signs of the present epoch.

In her turn, Czechoslovakia, sacrificed in September 1938 to Hitler's impatient lust for the peace

of the world and for a delusive hope of European
stabilization (as if imperialist appetites and the
principle of *international bad faith* could ever ad-
mit stabilization), was completely dismembered in
March 1939, and annexed as a protectorate country
of the German Empire.   By this act, the Reich has
crossed, so we may think, the threshold of the zone
where history's Eumenides waits for the conquerors
who are in too great a hurry.   So far as the destiny
of the Jews is concerned, the results of this annexation have been immediate.   The German racial
laws, with all their barbarism, are already in force
for the German populations of the Czech country;
and by contagion, the anti-Semitic mentality has
gained the entire former Czechoslovakian territory.

Due to German influence, intense anti-Semitism
also reigns in Hungary.   The Catholic episcopate
seeks to discourage enactment of the most violent
legislative measures, but anti-Jewish passion and
racist ideas have been unloosed.   One may say that
in persecuting the Jews, Hungary stands between
Germany and Italy.   Considering the situation occupied by Jews in commerce and industry, it appears
that German anti-Semitic propaganda pursues in

Hungary, as in Central Europe in general, the most concrete and precise aims, which is to ruin or enslave the industrial activity of these regions, and in reducing their national economies to a strictly agricultural status, to transform them into granaries for German needs.

What Must Be Done?

We have just seen to what excesses anti-Semitism has gone in various countries, revealing itself as one of the sinister symptoms of the general deterioration of our civilization, and ranging against the unfortunate and suffering, other men no less unfortunate and suffering.

In the face of such facts, is it possible to remain indifferent and inert? How can one escape the anxious question: *What must be done?* I realize that the world today resounds with the same question inspired by other horrors without number. But that is no reason for us to shut ourselves off. Everything must be done, every possible remedy tried, however insufficient each may seem by itself.

The president of the Polish Council, General Skladkowski, recently said: "In the name of the

Polish government I declare that we will oppose with all our might every pogrom and campaign of hatred such as arose last year against the Jews. There is no place among us for racial struggles. There is merely a problem of over-population, lying within the economic field alone." At the same time, the budget director of the Ministry of the Interior called on the colonial powers for "material and financial aid to Poland for the solution of the problem of Jewish emigration, with the cooperation of the Jews themselves." *

Emigration is therefore one of the proposed cures. To tell the truth, it would not, in the best case, be more than a partial remedy. It would bring some mitigation to the economic crisis of Eastern Europe by compensating, at least, for population increase resulting from births, perhaps even by cutting slightly the absolute total of the local Jewish population. The idea of mass emigration of all the Jews of Central and Eastern Europe is however absolutely out of the question because it is impossible.

But the tragedy is that, even reduced to these proportions and considered with reference only to

* *La Croix*, January 25, 1938.

a relatively small part of the Jewish population, emigration today faces major obstacles. All countries are closing their borders to emigrants. Here we are facing the general phenomenon so fatal to civilization, that of the turning in of nations upon themselves. As far as the Jews are concerned, Dr. Ruppin, professor at the Hebrew University of Jerusalem, observed some years ago that "the period of mass migrations, which transformed Jewish life during the last fifty years, must be regarded as closed. Emigration can at most take 30,000 to 40,000 Jews annually out of Eastern Europe, that is to say only one-third of their normal annual population increase in all the countries of Eastern Europe. One must ask whether, in such conditions, the economic position of the Jews in Eastern Europe, especially in Poland, is not threatened with veritable catastrophe since, during the last fifty years, emigration alone made it bearable." The same conclusion, then, is reached on the Jewish as on the Polish side.

Thus it would seem that, in the interests of all, the civilized community must take hold of itself. A special effort must be made, despite all obstacles, to facilitate some resumption, as large as possible, of Jewish emigration, that is, of voluntary emigration. And how? On the one hand, by means of Zionism, toward which, moreover, the Polish government has long shown itself favorable. But we realize the present difficulties in the Palestinian home, which can unfortunately take in only a small quota of immigrants. On the other hand, by having the nations, especially certain large nations possessing sparsely inhabited territories, resume a broader policy of immigration, thanks to an appropriate international organization; * the scanty generosity which certain countries, as for example Australia, have shown in this matter, is detrimental not only to Jews, but also to the common human family.

Finally, if necessary, settlement in certain colonial territories must be resorted to. That method

---

* For a general consideration of these problems, independent of the Jewish question, see *L'Homme Réel*, Feb.–March, 1936, and several articles by Magdeleine Paz and Madame Ancelet-Hustache. In France, a bill for a law concerning immigrants was filed on Dec. 11, 1934. Several law-decrees (*décrets-lois*) concerning foreigners were passed in 1938, but they do not go beyond the framework of police-measures, antecedent to a true policy of immigration. It must be observed that the figure of foreign population, due to political emigration from many European countries, amounts in France to about three million. This fact gives rise to serious problems.

presents special difficulties, due on one hand to the climatic conditions, often extremely bad, of some of the colonial lands intended for immigrants, and on the other hand, to the indispensable financial and economic equipment. I do not think, however, that these difficulties must be considered insurmountable. So far as France is concerned, the opening of Madagascar or of some other colonial territories, as for instance Guiana, to a fixed quota of Jewish emigrants has at times been suggested. I believe that if solid and well-elaborated offers were made in this direction to the French government (and no doubt these offers might be so conceived as to serve incidental national interests), this government would be disposed to examine them favorably. The same hope may be held in regard to the other colonial powers.*

German anti-Semitic policy has recently made the question of emigration still more urgent, although in

* If the demographic problem of Europe were considered in all its ramifications, one might be led to the idea of a general arrangement for the utilization and settlement of the vast colonization territories for the general benefit of the European and native populations. But such an idea would presuppose a true European community, and there again economics would appear to depend on morality and on politics.

reality, Jewish emigration has for Germany much less demographic interest than for Poland. But the aim was to improve her economic situation in bartering Jews for money or merchandise. Whatever these mercantile motives may be, it is the conflagration of hatred inflamed by German racism that renders the situation so full of anguish. If some world catastrophe does not alter radically and tragically the terms of all the problems of today, this question of Jewish emigration must be regarded as one which unconditionally requires a prompt solution for the entire West.

Here we must consider not simply the Jewish demographic problem in itself, but also the terrible threat which anti-Semitic passions, blindly encouraged by some governments, add to it. If it were possible now to bring forth and decide upon the absorption of a portion of the Jewish population over several decades, not only would a real if partial relief result for the Jewish and non-Jewish populations of eastern Europe, but perhaps there might transpire a sort of political and psychological purgation of anti-Semitic passions in the countries which are today in paroxysms.

I want to add that the insanity of anti-Semitism here displays itself strikingly: on the one hand, it persecutes the Jews in order to force them to emigrate, although the Jews have always provided a high percentage of emigrants and are prevented to-day only by a material obstacle, the general closing of frontiers. On the other hand, confirming a statement made at the outset of this essay, it adds one more obstacle to that emigration at which it aims, as well as to any real settlement of the Jewish problem. Because emigration, like any other settlement, presupposes the coöperation of the Jews themselves and hence an atmosphere of understanding and collaboration. In addition, it does not seem that the difficulties presented by emigration, particularly to colonial countries, could be solved under prevailing economic conditions of the various states, unless Jewish international welfare organizations were disposed to finance in part the settlement of emigrants who are without resources.

And yet, as far as anti-Semitic persecutions are concerned, the remedy we have been discussing, emigration, can at best be a mere palliative. Is there anything else to be considered? The fact remains that the great mass of the Jewish population must, in the best of cases, necessarily abide where it is. Millions of human beings cannot be expelled to become wanderers, men without a country. Are they to be driven to die of hunger? Are they all to be massacred? The more public opinion everywhere is informed and awakened, the more one can hope that persecution will lose ground. Legally, the Jewish populations may appeal to constitutional and international guarantees which have been extended to them. And it is up to the governments of countries to whom the word justice still has some meaning, to act, supported by public opinion, to compel respect for treaties which bear their signatures. The League of Nations, which showed itself so weak in many cases, took up the case of the Jews of Rumania during the Goga ministry. The United States has done much and can do much for the protection of the Jewish populations. The wave of indignation raised in the United States by the Nazi persecution in the fall of 1938 was formidable and accompanied by energetic action and efficacious measures of assistance, which merit the gratitude of all men of feeling.

And then?   Then one may hope that the entire
civilized world, if it succeeds in escaping a general
catastrophe, or perhaps having experienced one, will
come to know a fundamentally new and a more just
order.   For it seems that matters have reached a
pass where nothing can be remedied unless everything is transformed.   This conclusion, of course,
is one which brings little relief to those who are in
torment *today*.

There remains for all us, Jews and Christians, to
turn toward the invisible powers residing in the
heart of man, toward the springs of history which
lie within ourselves, in order to purify those springs.

If we but realized to what point external events
and the forms of things depend on the invisible pat-
terns which our free wills delineate within us, we
would have more confidence in spiritual means.

At the same time, we would renounce fighting
hatred with hatred.   We would understand what
has been so often affirmed by Gandhi, the real power
of love and truth even over political and social
realities.

Perhaps I may be allowed to address a special
appeal to our friends of Poland.   They know that

I have been careful to say nothing today which might wound them. If Poland manages to overcome, by a splendid rallying of its finest forces, the apparently irremediable conflicts to which the Jewish problem gives rise there, a great example will have been given to Europe.

According to the words of the President of the Polish Council which I just cited, there is no room among the Poles for racial conflicts. Would that they see that the union of all elements of the population is more essential for national prosperity than it is anywhere else. Would that they recall the declaration of Marshal Pilsudski on the reopening of the University of Warsaw, when he affirmed that, after having suffered oppression and persecution for more than a century, Poles could not harbor hatred for groups of different nationality and origin. There is a real problem in Poland, and it is above all economic and social, and its real solution is to be found in the advance of social justice and of economic equipment. On this road, the co-operation of the Jewish element is not to be underrated.

If they will dedicate the same energy to construction and invention as now goes into controversy, there would be a way for Jews and non-Jews to live on the same earth, perhaps in equal poverty, and to aid each other by brotherly labor. It has been said that "Jews and Poles must contrive to live together willy-nilly, since they are compelled to do so by fate." They will do so more profitably for the country if they arrange things *voluntarily*. Even with respect to economic categories, the problem here, too, is primarily of a moral order.

Polish Catholics, by entering deeply into the spirit of the reasons which have led their bishops, following the example of the Pope, to condemn Chauvinism, pagan Racism and anti-Semitism, along with Communism, will, it is hoped, understand that it is not enough to abstain from hating Jews as such in the heaven of spiritual feeling, while conceding to their enemies all the legends, the prejudices, the heated arguments in whose name they are persecuted on the earth of temporal realities, but that they must, responding to the general Christian and human vocation, descend with the grace of God and His justice to the very depths of mundane woes and conflicts, the very depths of this one as of all others!

Then will they give justice its hour, and many other things will come to pass in addition.

As to ourselves, wherever we are, we all bear responsibility to the extent that, as I just said, the drama of human history is like a visible projection of that which proceeds within ourselves. There is nothing more urgent than that secret labor by which those with *a little faith* raise, first of all in themselves, the level of mankind's spiritual energy. Such labor is effective, it brings forth tangible fruits more quickly than is realized.

There are in contemporary Europe those who, in order to fan the evil flame now consuming nations, are decreeing extermination and death, and first of all that of the Jews — because it is this they want, after all, is it not? There are those who, under the stupid apparatus of scientific Racism or forged documents, conceal from others and sometimes from themselves, a mad dream of a general massacre of the race of Moses and Jesus. While this massacre remains a dream, the germs of hate with which it pollutes the atmosphere are a reality. Much love, a great spirit of justice and charity, are required to cleanse that atmosphere.

Nowadays, for political ends, there is a remarkable abuse of names still dear to us, names in which even the most crushed of men still place hope. In some countries people "buy Christian" in order to boycott the Jewish merchant. Hating the Gospel, the dominant currents of German National Socialism proclaim themselves Christians — against the Pope and the churches. In Rumania Mr. Goga's party, if I am not mistaken, called itself National Christian, while that of Mr. Cuza was the League for Christian Defense. Perhaps some day there will be a Christian racism, perhaps Thors and Odins of Christian civilization, Christian mustard gas, and Christian bombardments of open cities. Men vie with each other as to who shall hound from this unhappy planet God's divinity, blasphemed by some, profaned by others. The despair into which many souls are in danger of being plunged by these things is heavy with malediction. It is not thus that Christian civilization can be defended. I do not believe that I am indulging in national self-satisfaction when I say that the Catholics of France heard with particular fervor what Pope Pius XI told their Bishops at Christmas 1937: "The preaching of the truth did not win many victories for Christ; it led to the Cross. It was by charity that he saved souls and led them to follow him." These words apply to Christians of the entire world. There is no other means for saving one's own soul, the souls of other men, and winning a modicum of peace for the world.

Our times offer to the demons of cruelty unheard-of banquets. Stalin gave them the Kulaks, Hitler gives them the Jews. Each one of us will have his turn perhaps. The immense clamor which arises from the German concentration camps as well as from the Russian is not perceptible to our ears, but it penetrates the secret fibres of the life of the world, and its invisible vibration tears them apart.

As to the anti-Semitic excesses of the fall of 1938 in Germany, the barbarity rose there to such a degree of cynicism that even in an age accustomed to the worst there came an explosion of general indignation. Nowhere was this explosion stronger than in the United States; this is an honor to this great country.

At the time that I was writing these lines the newspapers announced the formation of a council against anti-Semitism, consisting of fifty-two distinguished Americans of various faiths; this council came into existence "in response to the shocking persecution of Jews in Germany and in order to counteract organized attempts to introduce racial and religious intolerance in the United States." [1]   This enterprise will gladden the hearts of all those who think that in the increasing barbarization of humanity, the New Continent is perhaps destined to become one of the last ramparts of civilization.

When we learned that after a criminal assault, in itself absolutely reprehensible, committed in Paris against a secretary of the German embassy by a young Polish Jew frantic with trouble, the masters of German National-Socialism held all Jews responsible for the crime; that after having unloosed the so-called spontaneous violence of the populace, pillagings and pogroms, they condemned the German Jews, victims of these excesses, to pay the costs of the same; that they then imposed a collective fine equivalent to general expropriation, the purpose of which was to use international Jewish solidarity for the financial benefit of the persecutors of the Jews;

[1] *New York Times*, Nov. 28, 1938.

finally that practically the entire German Jewish population was going to be sentenced to slow death in revenge for a crime committed by one Jew against one Nazi; when we learned these things, we thought that truly armed men can do precisely what they will with unarmed men, we thought that we must thank the National-Socialists for not having decreed that all Jews today — and tomorrow, all Christians who prefer to obey God rather than men — be simply reduced to ashes by the most scientific means; for in the world of today who can stop them?

However, this is not entirely exact. The energetic American protest seems to have curbed the most savage plans formed by the racist persecution. Moreover, it is fitting to hail the moves undertaken by the United States, and the appeal made by it to civilized countries to come to the aid of the German Jews, to procure as rapidly as possible the emigration of the greatest possible number, to situate on an international basis the question of the Jewish minority in totalitarian countries.

In what way will this appeal be heard, and will these measures be successful? A primary obstacle is the economic and demographic difficulties raised by any relatively large emigration. Another obstacle is the collective egotism of nations.   As for the governments, will they have the courage to instill enough humanity into the administrative machinery that usually grinds without pity the weak and the poor? Driving back émigrés from the border, already done by some States, can only fill one with poignant sadness.   As for the people, will they still be sufficiently human to take upon themselves a little additional suffering in order to save their agonizing brothers from an earthly hell?

The day when President Roosevelt asked the prayers of all men of good will "for the unfortunate people in other lands who are in dire distress," * the day when confronted with the frightful impotence of the civilized world to assist such a throng of persecuted innocents, the head of a State thus turned toward heaven, he showed what are the real dimensions of the problem which disturbs today the conscience of nations.   For a time the unjust victors can do what they will; they themselves know that their time is short; this is the reason for their horrible haste.   If men are powerless to stop them,

* *New York Times*, Nov. 20, 1938.

a time will come when the voice of children will rise against them, a time will come when the anger of the elements and of inanimate beings will rise against them. For these stones from which God can raise up children to Abraham, He can also make cry out with indignation. And no matter how powerful the injustice of man be, nature and God are stronger still.

Never before in the history of the world were the Jews persecuted so universally; and never has persecution attacked, as today, both Jews and Christians. We can see here a sign that we have entered upon an apocalyptic period of history; this is also a sign that we must shape our means to the conditions of such a period. For a long time an all too human civilization put its trust in material forces, while invoking — and not always hypocritically — equity and the spirit. Today these material forces have been brought to the state of barbarism, and this is only the natural result of the perverted mentality which in its delusory belief that through them it could reign supreme, put everything in their power. In order to face the violence let loose in this way, men of freedom must not renounce the means which lay at their disposal in material energies, provided that these are subordinated to the spirit of justice; but they can no longer put their confidence in them, since the world itself summons them finally to put their trust in love and truth alone.